ANDREW MARVELL Poe

Andrew Marvell was born in
in Hull and Cambridge. He
Cromwell and in 1657 he too— ——... as the Latin
secretary to the Council of State. Famed as a satirist during his
lifetime, Marvell was a virtually unknown lyric poet until redis-
covered in the nineteenth century. However, it was only after
the First World War that his poetry gained popularity thanks
to the efforts of T. S. Eliot and Sir Herbert Grierson. Marvell
died in 1678.

Sean O'Brien is a poet, critic, broadcaster, editor and profes-
sor of creative writing at Newcastle University. His many books
include a verse version of Dante's *Inferno*, a novel, *Afterlife*,
and six prize-winning poetry collections. The most recent, *The
Drowned Book*, won both the Forward Prize and the T. S. Eliot
Prize in 2007.

ANDREW MARVELL
Poems selected by SEAN O'BRIEN

faber and faber

First published in 2010
by Faber and Faber Limited
Bloomsbury House, 74–77 Great Russell Street
London WC1B 3DA

Typeset by RefineCatch Ltd, Bungay, Suffolk
Printed in England by CPI BookMarque, Croydon

All rights reserved
Selection and Introduction © Sean O'Brien, 2010

The right of Sean O'Brien to be identified as editor
of this work has been asserted in accordance with Section 77
of the Copyright, Designs and Patents Act 1988

*This book is sold subject to the condition that it shall not,
by way of trade or otherwise, be lent, resold, hired out or
otherwise circulated without the publisher's prior consent
in any form of binding or cover other than that in which it
is published and without a similar condition including
this condition being imposed on the subsequent purchaser*

A CIP record for this book
is available from the British Library

ISBN 978–0–571–23548–3

10 9 8 7 6 5 4 3 2 1

Contents

Introduction

Insofar as poetry has a general readership, Andrew Marvell is a famous poet. His fame now rests mainly on two poems, 'An Horatian Ode upon Cromwel's Return from Ireland' and, much more emphatically, 'To His Coy Mistress'. Few readers, one suspects, venture much beyond 'The Garden'. The entire body of Marvell's work is very small, so that to make a selection from it is almost superfluous: but not quite, for Marvell will always deserve to be introduced.

Even among those unsympathetic to the relentlessly biographical tendency of our period, Marvell provokes interest because comparatively little about him can be stated with certainty. There are facts, but their meaning is often hard to establish, and it is hard to derive a consistent personality from them. As a recent editor, Nigel Smith, observes, 'Marvell was a secretive figure: in politics, he seems to have spared no effort to cover his tracks, even, allegedly, by leaving deliberately confusing false trails. In his correspondence, there is almost no discussion of literature, and poetry in particular.' The ability to adapt to changing political circumstances, which saw Marvell through the Civil War, the Commonwealth and the Restoration, was assisted by the fact that, while he became a noted controversialist in prose, little of his poetry was published in his lifetime. In a period such as our own, when electronic transmission often takes the place of manuscript circulation, his task might have been more difficult.

Born in rural East Yorkshire in 1621, Marvell grew up in Hull, attending the Grammar School. He graduated from Trinity College, Cambridge, in 1639. For several years during the Civil War he travelled in Europe. Moving in London literary circles on his return, he had Royalist connections and wrote commendatory verses for the leading Cavalier poet Richard Lovelace as well as an elegy for Francis Villiers, son of the Duke of Buckingham, killed in action in 1648. Yet in 1650, the year following the establishment of the Commonwealth, Marvell wrote 'An Horatian Ode' and in 1650–2 he served as tutor to Mary, child of the Parliamentarian general Sir Thomas Fairfax, a period which probably produced his most sustained poem, 'Upon Appleton House'. After serving as tutor to Oliver Cromwell's ward, in 1657 he followed Milton as Latin secretary to the council of state. In 1659 he became an MP for Hull, briefly losing his seat but regaining and holding it until his death, though said to have been a poor MP because of his ill temper. At the Restoration in 1660 he helped secure Milton's release from prison.

The 1660s saw Marvell travelling widely on political and diplomatic business. At the same time his work gained greater public attention as he turned to verse satire and to pamphleteering, latterly of an increasingly anti-Catholic tenor, which seems to have attracted the attention of the security services. He died in 1678, leaving his papers in the hands of his landlady Mary Palmer, who claimed to be his wife.

What Marvell thought, and what he felt, are open to inference, but there remains a persistent sense that he evades attention – perhaps because we want to give a stable form to a figure who seems always to be in movement. At times, patriotism notwithstanding, he appears sceptical about the nature and meaning of events and the springs of human conduct. The period in which he lived included a civil war and the execution of a king. As well as social and military turbulence, there was a torrent of debate in which precedent, justification and explanation for the world turned upside down were sought and passionately transmitted. He was not alone in the ideological distances he seems to have travelled, but his power to register the process, directly and otherwise, in his poems, is exceptional.

As Jonathan Bate has noted, Marvell's very name is hard to pin down. Like Shakespeare's, it appears in many forms. Nor is there agreement on its pronunciation: does the stress fall on the first or second syllable? Does it matter? Would Marvell have cared, or perhaps seen it as one more fruitful ambiguity? However we pronounce the name, Marvell might have been specially created for the age of criticism which was born with the development of English as an academic subject in the twentieth century. The weight and mass of critical attention to Marvell may appear spectacularly disproportionate to the quantity of work to which it is applied: only sixty-nine poems are firmly attributed to him. Yet though he wrote no epics and sought no poetic fame in his lifetime, Marvell has been one of the most written-about of poets – falling into the category of the great without having to be 'major' to attain it. That the interpretation of his work is in no sense settled has far more to do with the richness of the poems than with changes in critical fashion.

For many years most readers came to Marvell via Grierson's anthology *Metaphysical Poetry: Donne to Butler*, and latterly through Helen Gardner's Penguin anthology; the starting point for reading criticism in the field would usually be Eliot's famous essay 'The Metaphysical Poets' and the companion essay on Marvell himself. To Eliot are owed two very influential formulations. The first is the 'dissociation of sensibility' which Eliot claimed cut later poets off from their seventeenth-century predecessors, the likes of Donne and Marvell, who were able 'to devour any kind of experience' and create 'new wholes' from apparently unrelated phenomena. Thought thus belonged directly to the realm of experience and was not simply the abstracted reflection which Eliot contends it was later to become. The political baggage carried by the 'royalist, Anglo-Catholic, conservative' Eliot is well known: what this great critic is doing is generating a myth of considerable practical usefulness to himself; nevertheless his description of the poet at work 'transforming an observation into a state of mind' retains an urgent truth.

The second of Eliot's formulations characterises the quality of wit. In 'An Horatian Ode', Eliot says, it manifests itself as 'a tough reasonableness beneath the slight lyric grace'. More than this, we also find that the 'analytic' habit of Marvell's work, the process of scrutiny, is itself undergoing inspection in the making of the poem. Marvell's enduring appeal is partly a matter of the diversity of themes to which he applies this imaginative enquiry: love, politics, religion, elegy, philosophy, the pastoral and satire all engage him, and he rarely repeats himself. Perhaps still more important, though, is his use of argument and the appearance of argument to invoke states which transcend or even undermine the means by which and the basis on which they are broached. There is ultimately something mysterious in the poems – for example, the politics of 'An Horatian Ode', the tone of 'Little T.C.', the nature of the experience undergone and the understanding proposed in 'The Garden'. This is their great strength and is not to be confused with vagueness of the kind Eliot points out in the samples from the late Romantic William Morris which he uses for comparison.

The present selection was to have been made by the late Michael Donaghy, a poet whose affinity for the Metaphysicals is quickly apparent, but also one whose doubts about the susceptibility of experience to understanding, and even about its basic coherence, quickly become evident. Donaghy, like Marvell, was also fundamentally a dramatic poet, regarding the poem itself as an event of the imagination – hence his attachment to Marvell. The productive tension between experience and form brings to mind a comment by Lavinia Greenlaw with which Donaghy might well have agreed, that 'Poetry offers a coherence of sensation rather than meaning.'

Those who have taught Marvell's poems in the classroom will testify both to the difficulty of conveying this sense of event and to the liberating excitement it can produce for the reader who discovers the poetry's three-dimensional character. For example, in 'The Picture of Little T.C. in a Prospect of Flowers', the female child is imagined grown into a pitiless Diana, capable of breaking Cupid's bow:

O then let me in time compound,
And parly with those conquering Eyes;

> Ere they have try'd, their force to wound,
> Ere, with their glancing wheels, they drive
> In Triumph over Hearts that strive,
> And them that yield but more despise.
>   Let me be laid,
> Where I may see thy Glories from some Shade.

The pastoral and erotic elements here can naturally be paralleled in other poems of the period, but part of what gives 'Little T.C.' its peculiar and more than conventional impact is an urgency far beyond the conventional, a mood both tormented and excited. The hovering idea of a sexual transaction between speaker and child subject – something that stands worryingly in the offing for the present-day reader – is turned on its head, converted into the erotic extinction of the speaker. The triumph of Diana-like virginity is accompanied 'in prospect' by a strange compliant voyeurism from beyond the grave. This amounts to more than simply an ingenious manner of speaking; there is a more-than-conventional investment in the material. In 'Little T.C.' an immensely civilised imagination seems to encounter the limits of its own cultural and poetic categories, and the impact discharges a fascinated anxiety in which self-knowledge is both admitted and held at arm's length, as with asbestos gloves.

In the political sphere, in 'An Horatian Ode', something comparable appears to be taking place. The poem has provoked diametrically conflicting readings of its treatment of the execution of Charles I and the rise of Cromwell, which indicates how thoroughly dramatic it is in recreating the state of contradiction inhabited by many thoughtful observers of the events in question. At the same time as the poem seems to advocate the necessity of living with things are they are, not as they have been, it also appears to suggest that that pragmatist will have to accept that this political realism not only marks a violent breach in the traditions of kingship, but an undoing of the traditional hierarchy of nature itself:

Nature that hateth emptiness,
Allows of penetration less:
    And therefore must make room
    Where greater Spirits come.

Nature, according to this Republican sublime, must adapt to the
force of 'greater spirits' such as Cromwell; or it must retire alto-
gether, as a discarded model, in the face of their emergence. The
reserved elegance of the quatrain in which the transformation is
rendered carries the further implication that the world which is
to follow may well have no room for the imaginative assurance
which the poem itself embodies; if this is so, the conservative pes-
simism which some readers have sought to locate in the Horatian
Ode applies as much to its poetic and philosophical concerns as to
its political occasion. Later poets with political interests may look
with admiring envy at Marvell's conviction, however sombre, that
these are not separate realms but aspects of a single subject.

It is often too easy, too much the tired habit of the age, to sug-
gest that poet X is divided in himself – for example, in Marvell's
case, between affection for the courtly world of the old order
and an acknowledgement of implacable political necessity. To
read like this involves assumptions about subjectivity and sin-
cerity which, though embedded in our own period, may have
had different or lesser significance in others. Yet there is cer-
tainly a sense of friction in Marvell between the rich, sympa-
thetic delicacy of some of his imaginings (see 'Upon Appleton
House') and the brutal plainness he adopts elsewhere – for
example, in the famous lines from 'To His Coy Mistress': 'then
worms shall try / That long-preserv'd virginity.' It is hard to
miss the excited revulsion in the image, or the suggestion that
the mistress is in a sense already dead, 'preserved' as though
embalmed by her own moral rectitude. This tone, and the fact
that the mistress is present in the poem almost entirely in this
gynaecological sense, reveal a familiar and chilling form of male
intimidation. The intended act, and not the parties to it, are
the point: consummation and the extinction of desire will also

mark the extinction of loathing. In a sense, the poem never quite recovers from this calculated assault on its own powers of cajolery and persuasion:

> ... though we cannot make our sun
> Stand still, yet we will make him run.

The earlier image of Time's pursuing chariot might suggest that the lovers are running away from the declining sun, but Marvell's treatment of the traditional sex/death association may equally indicate that they take their course *towards* the sun, to face extinction head-on, so that in a sublime act of nihilism they challenge the sun to accelerate to meet them. Yet at the same time in this final couplet the speaker has reverted to a more character-istic elegant distance, delivering the allegedly logical conclusion as though it were a formality to be completed with negligent politeness while packing away the equipment. The intended effect might be to disarm resistance, but there is also a sense of disinvestment now that the way out is clear. While the poem is conspicuously situated in its genre – precedents can be found in Ovid and Catullus, and the *carpe diem* poem is of course a stock form of Marvell's age – Marvell's handling of convention provokes at least as much disquiet as recognition.

Though it is never less than interesting, some of Marvell's later work seems strangely crude, making it difficult to fol-low the imaginative arc from very early pieces like 'Eyes and Tears' and 'The Coronet'. It feels as if his true priorities have begun to lie elsewhere, that politics and religion have displaced poetry at the centre of his attention. The fact that this selec-tion is organised chronologically tends to emphasise this. But the remarkably high proportion of achieved poems remains, and the reader, once engaged – disturbed, intrigued, amused, amazed, tantalised – will return to Marvell's work at least as often as to that of the major poets in the canon.

SEAN O'BRIEN

ANDREW MARVELL

An Elegy upon the Death of My Lord Francis Villiers

Tis true that he is dead: but yet to chuse,
Methinkes thou Fame should not have brought the news.
Thou canst discourse at will and speak at large:
But wast not in the fight nor durst thou charge.
While he transported all with valiant rage
His Name eternizd, but cut short his age;
On the safe battlements of Richmonds bowers
Thou wast espyd, and from the guilded Towers
Thy silver Trumpets sounded a Retreat,
Farre from the dust and battails sulphry heat.
Yet what couldst thou have done? 'tis alwayes late
To struggle with inevitable fate.
Much rather thou I know expectst to tell
How heavy Cromwell gnasht the earth and fell.
Or how slow Death farre from the sight of day
The long-deceived Fairfax bore away.
But until then, let us young Francis praise:
And plant upon his hearse the bloody bayes,
Which we will water with our welling eyes.
Teares spring not still from spungy Cowardize.
The purer fountaines from the Rocks more steep
Destill and stony valour best doth weep.
Besides Revenge, if often quencht in teares,
Hardens like Steele and daily keener weares.

   Great Buckingham, whose death doth freshly strike
Our memoryes, because to this so like;
Ere that in the Eternall Court he shone,
And here a Favorite there found a throne;
The fatall night before he hence did bleed,
Left to his Princess this immortall seed.
As the wise Chinese in the fertile wombe
Of Earth doth a more precious clay entombe,
Which dying by his will he leaves consignd:

Til by mature delay of time refind
The christall metall fit to be releast
Is taken forth to crowne each royall feast:
Such was the fate by which this Postume breathd,
Who scarcely seems begotten but bequeathd.

   Never was any humane plant that grew
More faire than this and acceptably new.
'Tis truth that beauty doth most men dispraise:
Prudence and valour their esteeme do raise.
But he that hath already these in store,
Can not be poorer sure for having more.
And his unimitable handsomenesse
Made him indeed be more than man, not lesse.
We do but faintly Gods resemblance beare
And like rough coyns of carelesse mints appeare:
But he of purpose made, did represent
In a rich Medall every lineament.

   Lovely and admirable as he was,
Yet was his Sword or Armour all his Glasse.
Nor in his Mistris eyes that joy he tooke,
As in an Enemies himselfe to looke.
I know how well he did, with what delight
Those serious imitations of fight.
Still in the trialls of strong exercise
His was the first, and his the second prize.

   Bright Lady, thou that rulest from above
The last and greatest Monarchy of Love:
Faire Richmond hold thy Brother or he goes.
Try if the Jasmin of thy hand or Rose
Of thy red Lip can keep him alwayes here.
For he loves danger and doth never feare.
Or may thy tears prevaile with him to stay?

   But he resolv'd breaks carelesly away.
Onely one argument could now prolong
His stay and that most faire and so most strong:
The matchlesse Chlora whose pure fires did warm

4

His soule and only could his passions charme.
    You might with much more reason go reprove
The amorous Magnet which the North doth love.
Or preach divorce and say it is amisse
That with tall Elms the twining Vines should kisse
Then chide two such so fit, so equall faire
That in the world they have no other paire.
Whom it might seeme that Heaven did create
To restore man unto his first estate.
Yet she for honours tyrannous respect
Her own desires did and his neglect.
And like the Modest Plant at every touch
Shrunk in her leaves and feard it was too much.
    But who can paint the torments and that pain
Which he profest and now she could not faigne?
He like the Sun but overcast and pale:
Shee like a Rainbow, that ere long must faile,
Whose rosiall cheek where Heaven it selfe did view
Begins to separate and dissolve to dew.
    At last he leave obtaines though sad and slow,
First of her and then of himselfe to goe.
How comely and how terrible he sits
At once and Warre as well as Love befits!
Ride where thou wilt and bold adventures find:
But all the Ladies are got up behind.
Guard them, though not thy selfe: for in thy death
Th' Eleven thousand Virgins lose their breath.
    So Hector issuing from the Trojan wall
The sad Iliades to the Gods did call
With hands displayed and with dishevell'd haire
That they the Empire in his life would spare.
While he secure through all the field doth spy
Achilles, for Achilles only cry.
Ah ignorant that yet e're night he must
Be drawn by him inglorious through the dust.
    Such fell young Villiers in the chearfull heat

Of youth: his locks intangled all with sweat
And those eyes which the Sentinell did keep
Of love closed up in an eternall sleep.
While Venus of Adonis thinks no more
Slaine by the harsh tuske of the Savage Boare.
Hither she runns and hath him hurried farre
Out of the noise and blood, and killing warre:
Where in her Gardens of Sweet myrtle laid
Shee kisses him in the immortall shade,
   Yet dyed he not revengelesse: Much he did
Ere he could suffer. A whole Pyramid
Of Vulgar bodies he erected high:
Scorning without a Sepulcher to dye.
And with his steele which did whole troopes divide
He cut his Epitaph on either Side.
Till finding nothing to his courage fit
He rid up last to death and conquer'd it.
   Such are the Obsequies to Francis own:
He best the pompe of his owne death hath showne.
And we hereafter to his honour will
Not write so many, but so many kill.
Till the whole Army by just vengeance come
To be at once his Trophee and his Tombe.

To His Noble Friend Mr Richard Lovelace,
upon his Poems

Sir,
Our times are much degenerate from those
Which your sweet Muse, which your fair Fortune chose,
And as complexions alter with the Climes,
Our wits have drawne th' infections of our times.
That candid Age no other way could tell
To be ingenious, but by speaking well.
Who best could prayse, had then the greatest prayse,
'Twas more esteemed to give, than weare the Bayes:
Modest ambition studi'd only then,
To honour not her selfe, but worthy men.
These vertues now are banisht out of Towne,
Our Civill Wars have lost the Civicke crowne.
He highest builds, who with most Art destroys,
And against others Fame his owne employs.
I see the envious Caterpillar sit
On the faire blossome of each growing wit.

The Ayre's already tainted with the swarms
Of Insects which against you rise in arms.
Word-peckers, Paper-rats, Book-scorpions,
Of wit corrupted, the unfashion'd Sons.
The barbed Censurers begin to looke
Like the grim consistory on thy Booke:
And on each line cast a reforming eye,
Severer than the young Presbytery.
Till when in vaine they have thee all perus'd,
You shall for being faultless be accus'd.
Some reading your Lucasta, will alledge
You wrong'd in her the Houses Priviledge.
Some that you under sequestration are,
Because you write when going to the Warre,

And one the Book prohibits, because Kent
Their first Petition by the Authour sent.
    But when the beauteous Ladies came to know
That their deare Lovelace was endanger'd so:
Lovelace that thaw'd the most congealed brest,
He who lov'd best and them defended best.
Whose hand so rudely grasps the steely brand,
Whose hand so gently melts the Ladies hand.
They all in mutiny though yet undrest
Sally'd, and would in his defence contest.
And one the loveliest that was yet e're seen,
Thinking that I too of the rout had been.
Mine eyes invaded with a female spight,
(She knew what pain 'twould be to lose that sight.)
O no, mistake not, I reply'd, for I
In your defence, or in his cause would dy.
But he secure of glory and of time
Above their envy or mine aid doth clime.
Him, valiant men, and fairest Nymphs approve,
His Booke in them finds Judgement, with you Love.

On a Drop of Dew

See how the Orient Dew,
   Shed from the Bosom of the Morn
   Into the blowing Roses,
Yet careless of its Mansion new
For the clear Region where 'twas born,
   Round in its self incloses:
   And in its little Globes Extent,
Frames as it can its native Element.
   How it the purple flow'r does slight,
     Scarce touching where it lyes,
   But gazing back upon the Skies,
     Shines with a mournful Light;
       Like its own Tear,
Because so long divided from the Sphear.
   Restless it roules and unsecure,
     Trembling lest it grow impure:
   Till the warm Sun pitty it's Pain,
And to the Skies exhale it back again.
     So the Soul, that Drop, that Ray
Of the clear Fountain of Eternal Day,
Could it within the humane flow'r be seen,
     Remembering still its former height,
     Shuns the sweet leaves and blossoms green;
     And, recollecting its own Light,
Does, in its pure and circling thoughts, express
The greater Heaven in an Heaven less.
     In how coy a Figure wound,
     Every way it turns away:
     So the World excluding round,
     Yet receiving in the Day.
     Dark beneath, but bright above:
     Here disdaining, there in Love.
   How loose and easie hence to go:

How girt and ready to ascend.
Moving but on a point below,
It all about does upwards bend.
Such did the Manna's sacred Dew destil;
White, and intire, though congeal'd and chill.
Congeal'd on Earth: but does, dissolving, run
Into the Glories of th' Almighty Sun.

The Coronet

When for the Thorns with which I long, too long,
    With many a piercing wound,
    My Saviours head have crown'd,
I seek with Garlands to redress that Wrong;
    Through every Garden, every Mead,
I gather flow'rs (my fruits are only flow'rs)
    Dismantling all the fragrant Towers
That once adorn'd my Shepherdesses head.
And now when I have summ'd up all my store,
    Thinking (so I my self deceive)
    So rich a Chaplet thence to weave
As never yet the king of Glory wore:
    Alas I find the Serpent old
    That, twining in his speckled breast,
    About the flow'rs disguis'd does fold,
    With wreaths of Fame and Interest.
Ah, foolish Man, that would'st debase with them,
And mortal Glory, Heavens Diadem!
But thou who only could'st the Serpent tame,
Either his slipp'ry knots at once untie,
And disintangle all his winding Snare:
Or shatter too with him my curious frame:
And let these wither, so that he may die,
Though set with Skill and chosen out with Care.
That they, while Thou on both their Spoils dost tread,
May crown thy Feet, that could not crown thy Head.

Eyes and Tears

i

How wisely Nature did decree,
With the same Eyes to weep and see!
That, having view'd the object vain,
They might be ready to complain.

ii

And, since the Self-deluding Sight
In a false Angle takes each hight;
These Tears which better measure all,
Like wat'ry Lines and Plummets fall.

iii

Two Tears, which Sorrow long did weigh
Within the Scales of either Eye,
And then paid out in equal Poise,
Are the true price of all my Joyes.

iv

What in the World most fair appears,
Yea even Laughter, turns to Tears:
And all the Jewels which we prize,
Melt in these Pendants of the Eyes.

v

I have through every Garden been,
Amongst the Red, the White, the Green;
And yet, from all the flow'rs I saw,
No Hony, but these Tears could draw.

vi

So the all-seeing Sun each day
Distills the World with Chymick Ray;
But finds the Essence only Show'rs,
Which straight in pity back he poures.

vii

Yet happy they whom Grief doth bless,
That weep the more, and see the less:
And, to preserve their Sight more true,
Bath still their Eyes in their own Dew.

viii

So Magdalen, in Tears more wise
Dissolv'd those captivating Eyes,
Whose liquid Chaines could flowing meet
To fetter her Redeemers feet.

ix

Not full sailes hasting loaden home,
Nor the chast Ladies pregnant Womb,
Nor Cynthia Teeming show's so fair,
As two Eyes swoln with weeping are.

x

The sparkling Glance that shoots Desire,
Drench'd in these Waves, does lose its fire.
Yea oft the Thund'rer pitty takes
And here the hissing Lightning slakes.

xi

The Incense was to Heaven dear,
Not as a Perfume, but a Tear.
And Stars shew lovely in the Night,
But as they seem the Tears of Light.

xii

Ope then mine Eyes your double Sluice,
And practise so your noblest Use.
For others too can see, or sleep;
But only humane Eyes can weep.

xiii

Now like two Clouds dissolving, drop,
And at each Tear in Distance stop:

Now like two Fountains trickle down:
Now like two floods o'return and drown.

xiii

Thus let your Streams o'reflow your Springs,
Till Eyes and Tears be the same things:
And each the other's difference bears;
These weeping Eyes, those seeing Tears.

Bermudas

Where the remote Bermudas ride
In th' Oceans bosome unespy'd,
From a small Boat, that row'd along,
The listning Winds receiv'd this Song.

    What should we do but sing his Praise
That led us through the watry Maze,
Unto an Isle so long unknown,
And yet far kinder than our own?
Where he the huge Sea-Monsters wracks,
That lift the Deep upon their Backs.
He lands us on a grassy Stage;
Safe from the Storms, and Prelat's rage.
He gave us this eternal Spring,
Which here enamells every thing;
And sends the Fowl's to us in care,
On daily Visits through the Air.
He hangs in shades the Orange bright,
Like golden Lamps in a green Night.
And does in the Pomgranates close
Jewels more rich than Ormus shows.
He makes the Figs our mouths to meet;
And throws the Melons at our feet.
But Apples plants of such a price,
No Tree could ever bear them twice.
With Cedars, chosen by his hand,
From Lebanon, he stores the Land.
And makes the hollow Seas, that roar,
Proclaime the Ambergris on shoar.
He cast (of which we rather boast)
The Gospels Pearl upon our Coast.
And in these Rocks for us did frame
A Temple, where to sound his Name.
Oh let our Voice his Praise exalt,

Till it arrive at Heavens Vault:
Which thence (perhaps) rebounding, may
Eccho beyond the Mexique Bay.
Thus sung they, in the English boat,
An holy and a chearful Note,
And all the way, to guide their Chime,
With falling Oars they kept the time.

Clorinda and Damon

C. Damon come drive thy flocks this way.
D. No: 'tis too late they went astray.
C. I have a grassy Scutcheon spy'd,
   Where Flora blazons all her pride.
   The Grass I aim to feast thy Sheep:
   The Flow'rs I for thy Temples keep.
D. Grass withers; and the Flow'rs too fade.
C. Seize the short Joyes then, ere they vade.
   Seest thou that unfrequented Cave?
D. That den? C. Loves Shrine. D. But Virtue's Grave.
C. In whose cool bosome we may lye
   Safe from the Sun. D. Not Heaven's Eye.
C. Near this, a Fountaines liquid Bell
   Tinkles within the concave Shell.
D. Might a Soul bath there and be clean,
   Or slake its Drought? C. What is't you mean?
D. These once had been enticing things,
   Clorinda, Pastures, Caves, and Springs.
C. And what late change? D. The other day
   Pan met me. C. What did great Pan say?
D. Words that transcend poor Shepherds skill;
   But He e'er since my Songs does fill:
   And his Name swells my slender Oate.
C. Sweet must Pan sound in Damons Note.
D. Clorinda's voice might make it sweet.
C. Who would not in Pan's Praises meet?

Chorus
Of Pan the flowry Pastures sing,
Caves eccho, and the Fountains ring.
Sing then while he doth us inspire;
For all the World is our Pan's Quire.

A Dialogue between the Soul and Body

Soul

   O Who shall, from this Dungeon, raise
A Soul enslav'd so many wayes?
With bolts of Bones, that fetter'd stands
In Feet; and manacled in Hands.
Here blinded with an Eye; and there
Deaf with the drumming of an Ear.
A Soul hung up, as 'twere, in Chains
Of Nerves, and Arteries, and Veins.
Tortur'd, besides each other part,
In a vain Head, and double Heart.

Body

   O who shall me deliver whole,
From bonds of this Tyrannic Soul?
Which, stretcht upright, impales me so,
That mine own Precipice I go;
And warms and moves this needless Frame:
(A Fever could but do the same.)
And, wanting where its spight to try,
Has made me live to let me dye.
A Body that could never rest,
Since this ill Spirit it possest.

Soul

   What Magick could me thus confine
Within anothers Grief to pine?
Where whatsoever it complain,
I feel, that cannot feel, the pain.
And all my Care its self employes,
That to preserve, which me destroys:
Constrain'd not only to indure
Diseases, but, whats worse, the Cure:

And ready oft the Port to gain,
Am Shipwrackt into Health again.

Body
   But Physick yet could never reach
The Maladies Thou me dost teach;
Whom first the Cramp of Hope does Tear:
And then the Palsie Shakes of Fear.
The Pestilence of Love does heat:
Or Hatred's hidden Ulcer eat.
Joy's chearful Madness does perplex:
Or Sorrow's other Madness vex.
Which Knowledge forces me to know;
And Memory will not foregoe.
What but a Soul could have the wit
To build me up for Sin so fit?
So Architects do square and hew
Green Trees that in the Forest grew.

The Definition of Love

i

My Love is of a birth as rare
As 'tis for object strange and high:
It was begotten by despair
Upon Impossibility.

ii

Magnanimous Despair alone
Could show me so divine a thing,
Where feeble Hope could ne'r have flown
But vainly flapt its Tinsel Wing.

iii

And yet I quickly might arrive
Where my extended Soul is fixt,
But Fate does Iron wedges drive,
And alwaies crouds it self betwixt.

iv

For Fate with jealous Eye does see
Two perfect Loves; nor lets them close;
Their union would her ruine be,
And her Tyrannick pow'r depose.

v

And therefore her Decrees of Steel
Us as the distant Poles have plac'd,
(Though Loves whole World on us doth wheel)
Not by themselves to be embrac'd.

vi

Unless the giddy Heaven fall,
And Earth some new Convulsion tear;
And, us to joyn, the World should all
Be cramp'd into a Planisphere.

vii

As Lines so Loves oblique may well
Themselves in every Angle greet:
But ours so truly Paralel,
Though infinite can never meet.

viii

Therefore the Love which us doth bind,
But Fate so enviously debarrs,
Is the Conjunction of the Mind,
And Opposition of the Stars.

Daphnis and Chloe

i

Daphnis must from Chloe part:
Now is come the dismal Hour
That must all his Hopes devour,
All his Labour, all his Art.

ii

Nature, her own Sexes foe,
Long had taught her to be coy:
But she neither knew t'enjoy,
Nor yet let her Lover go.

iii

But, with this sad News surpriz'd
Soon she let that Niceness fall;
And would gladly yield to all,
So it had his stay compriz'd.

iv

Nature so her self does use
To lay by her wonted State,
Lest the World should separate;
Sudden Parting closer glews.

v

He, well read in all the wayes
By which men their Siege maintain,
Knew not that the Fort to gain
Better 'twas the Siege to raise.

vi

But he came so full possest
With the Grief of Parting thence,
That he had not so much Sence
As to see he might be blest.

vii

Till Love in her Language breath'd
Words she never spake before;
But than Legacies no more
To a dying Man bequeath'd.

viii

For, Alas, the time was spent,
Now the latest minut's run
When poor Daphnis is undone,
Between Joy and Sorrow rent.

ix

At that Why, that Stay my Dear,
His disorder'd Locks he tare;
And with rouling Eyes did glare,
And his cruel Fate forswear.

x

As the Soul of one scarce dead,
With the shrieks of Friends aghast,
Looks distracted back in hast,
And then streight again is fled.

xi

So did wretched Daphnis look,
Frighting her he loved most.
At the last, this Lovers Ghost
Thus his Leave resolved took.

xii

Are my Hell and Heaven Joyn'd
More to torture him that dies?
Could departure not suffice,
But that you must then grow kind?

xiii

Ah my Chloe how have I
Such a wretched minute found,

When thy Favours should me wound
More than all thy Cruelty?

xiv

So to the condemned Wight
The delicious Cup we fill;
And allow him all he will,
For his last and short Delight.

xv

But I will not now begin
Such a Debt unto my Foe;
Nor to my Departure owe
What my Presence could not win.

xvi

Absence is too much alone:
Better 'tis to go in peace,
Than my Losses to increase
By a late Fruition.

xvii

Why should I enrich my Fate?
'Tis a Vanity to wear,
For my Executioner,
Jewels of so high a rate.

xviii

Rather I away will pine
In a manly stubborness
Than be fatted up express
For the Canibal to dine.

xix

Whilst this grief does thee disarm,
All th' Enjoyment of our Love
But the ravishment would prove
Of a Body dead while warm.

xx

And I parting should appear
Like the Gourmand Hebrew dead,
While with Quailes and Manna fed,
He does through the Desert err;

xxi

Or the Witch that midnight wakes
For the Fern, whose magick Weed
In one minute casts the Seed,
And invisible him makes.

xxii

Gentler times for Love are ment:
Who for parting pleasure strain
Gather Roses in the rain,
Wet themselves and spoil their Scent.

xxiii

Farewell therefore all the fruit
Which I could from Love receive:
Joy will not with Sorrow weave,
Nor will I this Grief pollute.

xxiv

Fate I come, as dark, as sad,
As thy Malice could desire;
Yet bring with me all the Fire
That Love in his Torches had.

xxv

At these words away he broke;
As who long has praying ly'n,
To his Heads-man makes the Sign,
And receives the parting stroke.

xxvi

But hence Virgins all beware.
Last night he with Phlogis slept;

This night for Dorinda kept;
And but rid to take the Air.

xxvii

Yet he does himself excuse,
Nor indeed without a Cause.
For, according to the Lawes,
Why did Chloe once refuse?

To His Coy Mistress

    Had we but World enough, and Time,
This coyness Lady were no crime.
We would sit down, and think which way
To walk, and pass our long Loves Day.
Thou by the Indian Ganges side
Should'st Rubies find: I by the Tide
Of Humber would complain. I would
Love you ten years before the Flood:
And you should, if you please, refuse
Till the Conversion of the Jews.
My vegetable Love should grow
Vaster than Empires, and more slow.
An hundred years should go to praise
Thine Eyes, and on thy Forehead Gaze.
Two hundred to adore each Breast:
But thirty thousand to the rest.
An Age at least to every part,
And the last Age should show your Heart.
For Lady you deserve this State;
Nor would I love at lower rate.
    But at my back I alwaies hear
Times winged Charriot hurrying near:
And yonder all before us lye
Deserts of vast Eternity.
Thy Beauty shall no more be found;
Nor, in thy marble Vault, shall sound
My ecchoing Song: then Worms shall try
That long preserv'd Virginity:
And your quaint Honour turn to dust;
And into ashes all my Lust.
The Grave's a fine and private place,
But none I think do there embrace.
    Now therefore, while the youthful hew

Sits on thy skin like morning glew,
And while thy willing Soul transpires
At every pore with instant Fires,
Now let us sport us while we may;
And now, like am'rous birds of prey,
Rather at once our Time devour,
Than languish in his slow-chapt pow'r.
Let us roll all our Strength, and all
Our sweetness, up into one Ball:
And tear our Pleasures with rough strife,
Thorough the Iron gates of Life.
Thus, though we cannot make our Sun
Stand still, yet we will make him run.

The Picture of Little T. C. in a Prospect of Flowers

i

See with what simplicity
This Nimph begins her golden daies!
In the green Grass she loves to lie,
And there with her fair Aspect tames
The Wilder flow'rs, and gives them names:
But only with the Roses playes;
       And them does tell
What Colour best becomes them, and what Smell.

ii

Who can foretel for what high cause
This Darling of the Gods was born!
Yet this is She whose chaster Laws
The wanton Love shall one day fear,
And, under her command severe,
See his Bow broke and Ensigns torn.
       Happy, who can
Appease this virtuous Enemy of Man!

iii

O then let me in time compound,
And parly with those conquering Eyes;
Ere they have try'd their force to wound,
Ere, with their glancing wheels, they drive
In Triumph over Hearts that strive,
And them that yield but more despise.
       Let me be laid,
Where I may see thy Glories from some Shade.

iv

Mean time, whilst every verdant thing
It self does at thy Beauty charm,
Reform the errours of the Spring;

Make that the Tulips may have share
Of sweetness, seeing they are fair;
And Roses of their thorns disarm:
> But most procure
That Violets may a longer Age endure.

v

But O young beauty of the Woods,
Whom Nature courts with fruits and flow'rs,
Gather the Flow'rs, but spare the Buds;
Lest Flora angry at thy crime,
To kill her Infants in their prime,
Do quickly make th' Example Yours;
> And, ere we see,
Nip in the blossome all our hopes and Thee.

The Mower against Gardens

Luxurious Man, to bring his Vice in use,
　　Did after him the World seduce:
And from the fields the Flow'rs and Plants allure,
　　Where Nature was most plain and pure.
He first enclos'd within the Gardens square
　　A dead and standing pool of Air:
And a more luscious Earth for them did knead,
　　Which stupifi'd them while it fed.
The Pink grew then as double as his Mind;
　　The nutriment did change the kind.
With strange perfumes he did the Roses taint,
　　And Flow'rs themselves were taught to paint.
The Tulip, white, did for complexion seek;
　　And learn'd to interline its cheek:
Its Onion root they then so high did hold,
　　That one was for a Meadow sold.
Another World was search'd, through Oceans new,
　　To find the Marvel of Peru.
And yet these Rarities might be allow'd,
　　To Man, that sov'raign thing and proud;
Had he not dealt between the Bark and Tree,
　　Forbidden mixtures there to see.
No Plant now knew the Stock from which it came;
　　He grafts upon the Wild the Tame:
That the uncertain and adult'rate fruit
　　Might put the Palate in dispute.
His green Seraglio has its Eunuchs too;
　　Lest any Tyrant him out-doe.
And in the Cherry he does Nature vex,
　　To procreate without a Sex.
'Tis all enforc'd; the Fountain and the Grot;
　　While the sweet Fields do lye forgot:
Where willing Nature does to all dispence

A wild and fragrant Innocence:
And Fauns and Faryes do the Meadows till,
 More by their presence than their skill.
Their Statues polish'd by some ancient hand,
 May to adorn the Gardens stand:
But howso'ere the Figures do excel,
 The Gods themselves with us do dwell.

Damon the Mower

i

Heark how the Mower Damon Sung,
With love of Juliana stung!
While ev'ry thing did seem to paint
The Scene more fit for his complaint.
Like her fair Eyes the day was fair;
But scorching like his am'rous Care.
Sharp like his Sythe his Sorrow was,
And wither'd like his Hopes the Grass.

ii

Oh what unusual Heats are here,
Which thus our Sun-burn'd Meadows fear!
The Grass-hopper its pipe gives ore;
And hamstring'd Frogs can dance no more.
But in the brook the green Frog wades;
And Grass-hoppers seek out the shades.
Only the Snake, that kept within,
Now glitters in its second skin.

iii

This heat the Sun could never raise,
Nor Dog-star so inflame's the dayes.
It from an higher Beauty grow'th,
Which burns the Fields and Mower both:
Which mads the Dog, and makes the Sun
Hotter than his own Phaeton.
Not July causeth these Extremes,
But Juliana's scorching beams.

iv

Tell me where I may pass the Fires
Of the hot day, or hot desires.
To what cool Cave shall I descend,
Or to what gelid Fountain bend?

Alas! I look for Ease in vain,
When Remedies themselves complain.
No moisture but my Tears do rest,
Nor Cold but in her Icy Breast.

v

How long wilt Thou, fair Shepheardess,
Esteem me, and my Presents less?
To Thee the harmless Snake I bring,
Disarmed of its teeth and sting.
To Thee Chameleons changing-hue,
And Oak leaves tipt with hony-dew.
Yet Thou ungrateful hast not sought
Nor what they are, nor who them brought.

vi

I am the Mower Damon, known
Through all the Meadows I have mown.
On me the Morn her dew distills
Before her darling Daffadils.
And, if at Noon my toil me heat,
The Sun himself licks off my Sweat.
While, going home, the Ev'ning sweet
In cowslip-water bathes my feet.

vii

What, though the piping Shepherd stock
The plains with an unnumber'd Flock,
This Sithe of mine discovers wide
More ground than all his Sheep do hide.
With this the golden fleece I shear
Of all these Closes ev'ry Year.
And though in Wooll more poor than they,
Yet am I richer far in Hay.

viii

Nor am I so deform'd to sight,
If in my Sithe I looked right;

In which I see my Picture done,
As in a crescent Moon the Sun.
The deathless Fairyes take me oft
To lead them in their Danses soft:
And, when I tune my self to sing,
About me they contract their Ring.

ix

How happy might I still have mow'd,
Had not Love here his Thistles sow'd!
But now I all the day complain,
Joyning my Labour to my Pain;
And with my Sythe cut down the Grass,
Yet still my Grief is where it was:
But, when the Iron blunter grows,
Sighing I whet my Sythe and Woes.

x

While thus he threw his Elbow round,
Depopulating all the Ground,
And, with his whistling Sythe, does cut
Each stroke between the Earth and Root,
The edged Stele by careless chance
Did into his own Ankle glance;
And there among the Grass fell down,
By his own Sythe, the Mower mown.

xi

Alas! said He, these hurts are slight
To those that dye by Loves despight.
With Shepherds-purse, and Clowns-all-heal,
The Blood I stanch, and Wound I seal.
Only for him no Cure is found,
Whom Julianas Eyes do wound.
'Tis death alone that this must do:
For Death thou art a Mower too.

The Mower to the Glow-worms

i

Ye living Lamps, by whose dear light
The Nightingale does sit so late,
And studying all the Summer-night,
Her matchless Songs does meditate;

ii

Ye Country Comets, that portend
No War, nor Princes funeral,
Shining unto no higher end
Than to presage the Grasses fall;

iii

Ye Glow-worms, whose officious Flame
To wandring Mowers shows the way,
That in the Night have lost their aim,
And after foolish Fires do stray;

iv

Your courteous Lights in vain you waste,
Since Juliana here is come,
For She my Mind hath so displac'd
That I shall never find my home.

The Garden

i

How vainly men themselves amaze
To win the Palm, the Oke, or Bayes;
And their uncessant Labours see
Crown'd from some single Herb or Tree,
Whose short and narrow verged Shade
Does prudently their Toyles upbraid;
While all Flow'rs and all Trees do close
To weave the Garlands of repose.

ii

Fair quiet, have I found thee here,
And Innocence thy Sister dear!
Mistaken long, I sought you then
In busie Companies of Men.
Your sacred Plants, if here below,
Only among the Plants will grow.
Society is all but rude,
To this delicious Solitude.

iii

No white nor red was ever seen
So am'rous as this lovely green.
Fond Lovers, cruel as their Flame,
Cut in these Trees their Mistress name.
Little, Alas, they know, or heed,
How far these Beauties Hers exceed!
Fair Trees! where s'ere your barkes I wound,
No Name shall but your own be found.

iv

When we have run our Passions heat,
Love hither makes his best retreat.
The Gods, that mortal Beauty chase,
Still in a Tree did end their race.

Apollo hunted Daphne so,
Only that She might Laurel grow.
And Pan did after Syrinx speed,
Not as a Nymph, but for a Reed.

v

What wond'rous Life in this I lead!
Ripe Apples drop about my head;
The Luscious Clusters of the Vine
Upon my Mouth do crush their Wine;
The Nectaren, and curious Peach,
Into my hands themselves do reach;
Stumbling on Melons, as I pass,
Insnar'd with Flow'rs, I fall on Grass.

vi

Mean while the Mind, from pleasures less,
Withdraws into its happiness:
The Mind, that Ocean where each kind
Does streight its own resemblance find;
Yet it creates, transcending these,
Far other Worlds, and other Seas;
Annihilating all that's made
To a green Thought in a green Shade.

vii

Here at the Fountains sliding foot,
Or at some Fruit-tree's mossy root,
Casting the Bodies Vest aside,
My Soul into the boughs does glide:
There like a Bird it sits, and sings,
Then whets, and combs its silver Wings;
And, till prepar'd for longer flight,
Waves in its Plumes the various Light.

viii

Such was that happy Garden-state,
While Man there walk'd without a Mate:

After a Place so pure, and sweet,
What other Help could yet be meet!
But 'twas beyond a Mortal's share
To wander solitary there:
Two Paradises 'twere in one
To live in Paradise alone.

ix

How well the skilful Gardner drew
Of flow'rs and herbes this Dial new;
Where from above the milder Sun
Does through a fragrant Zodiack run;
And, as it works, th' industrious Bee
Computes its time as well as we.
How could such sweet and wholsome Hours
Be reckon'd but with herbs and flow'rs!

from Upon Appleton House

To My Lord Fairfax

xxxviii

These, as their Governour goes by,
In fragrant Vollyes they let fly;
And to salute their Governess
Again as great a charge they press:
None for the Virgin Nymph; for She
Seems with the Flow'rs a Flow'r to be.
And think so still! though not compare
With Breath so sweet, or Cheek so faire.

xxxix

Well shot ye Firemen! Oh how sweet,
And round your equal Fires do meet;
Whose shrill report no Ear can tell,
But Ecchoes to the Eye and smell.
See how the Flow'rs, as at Parade,
Under their Colours stand displaid:
Each Regiment in order grows,
That of the Tulip, Pinke, and Rose.

xl

But when the vigilant Patroul
Of Stars walks round about the Pole,
Their Leaves, that to the stalks are curl'd,
Seem to their Staves the Ensigns furl'd.
Then in some Flow'rs beloved Hut
Each Bee as Sentinel is shut;
And sleeps so too: but, if once stir'd,
She runs you through, nor askes the Word.

xli

Oh Thou, that dear and happy Isle
The Garden of the World ere while,

Thou Paradise of four Seas,
Which Heaven planted us to please,
But, to exclude the World, did guard
With watry if not flaming Sword;
What luckless Apple did we taste,
To make us Mortal, and Thee Waste?

xlii

Unhappy! shall we never more
That sweet Militia restore,
When Gardens only had their Towrs,
And all the Garrisons were Flowrs,
When Roses only Arms might bear,
And Men did rosie Garlands wear?
Tulips, in several Colours barr'd,
Were then the Switzers of our Guard.

xliii

The Gardiner had the Souldiers place,
And his more gentle Forts did trace.
The Nursery of all things green
Was then the only Magazeen.
The Winter Quarters were the Stoves,
Where he the tender Plants removes.
But War all this doth overgrow:
We Ord'nance Plant and Powder sow.

xliv

And yet there walks one on the Sod
Who, had it pleased him and God,
Might once have made our Gardens spring
Fresh as his own and flourishing.
But he preferr'd to the Cinque Ports
These five imaginary Forts:
And, in those half-dry Trenches, spann'd
Pow'r which the Ocean might command.

xlv

For he did, with his utmost Skill,
Ambition weed, but Conscience till.
Conscience, that Heaven-nursed Plant,
Which most our Earthly Gardens want.
A prickling leaf it bears, and such
As that which shrinks at ev'ry touch;
But Flowrs eternal, and divine,
That in the Crowns of Saints do shine.

xlvi

The sight does from these Bastions ply,
Th' invisible Artilery;
And at proud Cawood-Castle seems
To point the Battery of its Beams.
As if it quarrell'd in the Seat
Th' Ambition of its Prelate great.
But ore the Meads below it plays,
Or innocently seems to gaze.

xlvii

And now to the Abbyss I pass
Of that unfathomable Grass,
Where Men like Grashoppers appear,
But Grashoppers are Gyants there:
They, in there squeaking Laugh, contemn
Us as we walk more low than them:
And, from the Precipices tall
Of the green spires, to us do call.

xlviii

To see Men through this Meadow Dive,
We wonder how they rise alive.
As, under Water, none does know
Whether he fall through it or go.
But, as the Marriners that sound,
And show upon their Lead the Ground,

They bring up Flow'rs so to be seen,
And prove they've at the Bottom been.

xlix

No Scene that turns with Engines strange
Does oftner than these Meadows change.
For when the Sun the Grass hath vext,
The tawny Mowers enter next;
Who seem like Israelites to be,
Walking on foot through a green Sea.
To them the Grassy Deeps divide,
And crowd a Lane to either Side.

l

With whistling Sithe, and Elbow strong,
These Massacre the Grass along:
While one, unknowing, carves the Rail,
Whose yet unfeather'd Quils her fail.
The Edge all bloody from its Breast
He draws, and does his stroke detest;
Fearing the Flesh untimely mow'd
To him a Fate as black forebode.

li

But bloody Thestylis, that waites
To bring the mowing Camp their Cates,
Greedy as Kites has trust it up,
And forthwith means on it to sup:
When on another quick She lights,
And cryes, 'He call'd us Israelites;
But now, to make his saying true,
Rails rain for Quails, for Manna Dew.'

lii

Unhappy Birds! what does it boot
To build below the Grasses Root;
When Lowness is unsafe as Hight,
And Chance o'retakes what scapeth spight?

And now your Orphan Parents Call
Sounds your untimely Funeral.
Death Trumpets creak in such a Note,
And 'tis the Sourdine in their Throat.

liii

Or sooner hatch or higher build:
The Mower now commands the Field;
In whose new Traverse seemeth wrought
A Camp of Battail newly fought:
Where, as the Meads with Hay, the Plain
Lyes quilted ore with Bodies slain:
The Women that with forks it fling,
Do represent the Pillaging.

liv

And now the careless Victors play,
Dancing the Triumphs of the Hay;
Where every Mowers wholesome Heat
Smells like an Alexanders sweat.
Their Females fragrant as the Mead
Which they in Fairy Circles tread:
When at their Dances End they kiss,
Their new-made Hay not sweeter is.

lv

When after this 'tis pil'd in Cocks,
Like a calm Sea it shews the Rocks:
We wondring in the River near
How Boats among them safely steer.
Or, like the Desert Memphis Sand,
Short Pyramids of Hay do stand.
And such the Roman Camps do rise
In Hills for Soldiers Obsequies.

lvi

This Scene again withdrawing brings
A new and empty Face of things;

A levell'd space, as smooth and plain,
As Clothes for Lilly strecht to stain.
The World when first created sure
Was such a Table rase and pure.
Or rather such is the Toril
Ere the Bulls enter at Madril.

lvii
For to this naked equal Flat,
Which Levellers take Pattern at,
The Villagers in common chase
Their Cattle, which it closer rase;
And what below the Scythe increast
Is pincht yet nearer by the Beast.
Such, in the painted World, appear'd
Davenant with th' Universal Heard.

lviii
They seem within the polisht Grass
A Landskip drawen in Looking-Glass.
And shrunk in the huge Pasture show
As Spots, so shap'd, on Faces do.
Such Fleas, ere they approach the Eye,
In Multiplying Glasses lye.
They feed so wide, so slowly move,
As Constellations do above.

lix
Then, to conclude these pleasant Acts,
Denton sets ope its Cataracts;
And makes the Meadow truly be
(What it but seem'd before) a Sea.
For, jealous of its Lords long stay,
It try's t'invite him thus away.
The River in it self is drown'd,
And Isles th' astonisht Cattle round.

lx

Let others tell the Paradox,
How Eels now bellow in the Ox;
How Horses at their Tails do kick,
Turn'd as they hang to Leeches quick;
How Boats can over Bridges sail;
And Fishes do the Stables scale.
How Salmons trespassing are found;
And Pikes are taken in the Pound.

     .   .   .   .   .   .

lxxxii

But now away my Hooks, my Quills,
And Angles, idle Utensils.
The young Maria walks to night:
Hide trifling Youth thy Pleasures slight.
'Twere shame that such judicious Eyes
Should with such Toyes a Man surprize;
She that already is the Law
Of all her Sex, her Ages Aw.

lxxxiii

See how loose Nature, in respect
To her, it self doth recollect;
And every thing so whisht and fine,
Starts forthwith to its Bonne Mine.
The Sun himself, of Her aware,
Seems to descend with greater Care;
And lest She see him go to Bed,
In blushing Clouds conceales his Head.

lxxxiv

So when the Shadows laid asleep
From underneath these Banks do creep,
And on the River as it flows
With Eben Shuts begin to close;
The modest Halcyon comes in sight,

Flying betwixt the Day and Night;
And such an horror calm and dumb,
Admiring Nature does benum.

lxxxv
The viscous Air, wheres'ere She fly,
Follows and sucks her Azure dy;
The gellying Stream compacts below,
If it might fix her shadow so;
The stupid Fishes hang, as plain
As Flies in Chrystal overt'ane;
And Men the silent Scene assist,
Charm'd with the Saphir-winged Mist.

lxxxvi
Maria such, and so doth hush
The World, and through the Ev'ning rush.
No new-born Comet such a Train
Draws through the Skie, nor Star new-slain.
For streight those giddy Rockets fail,
Which from the putrid Earth exhale,
But by her Flames, in Heaven try'd,
Nature is wholly vitrifi'd.

lxxxvii
'Tis She that to these Gardens gave
That wondrous Beauty which they have;
She streightness on the Woods bestows;
To Her the Meadow sweetness owes;
Nothing could make the River be
So Chrystal-pure but only She;
She yet more Pure, Sweet, Streight, and Fair,
Than Gardens, Woods, Meads, Rivers are.

lxxxviii
Therefore what first She on them spent,
They gratefully again present.
The Meadow Carpets where to tread;

The Garden Flow'rs to Crown Her Head;
And for a Glass the limpid Brook,
Where She may all her Beautyes look;
But, since She would not have them seen,
The Wood about her draws a Skreen.

lxxxix
For She; to higher Beauties rais'd,
Disdains to be for lesser prais'd.
She counts her Beauty to converse
In all the Languages as hers;
Nor yet in those her self imployes
But for the Wisdome, not the Noyse;
Nor yet that Wisdome would affect,
But as 'tis Heavens Dialect.

lxxxx
Blest Nymph! that couldst so soon prevent
Those Trains by Youth against thee meant;
Tears (watry Shot that pierce the Mind;)
And Sighs (Loves Cannon charg'd with Wind;)
True Praise (That breaks through all defence;)
And feign'd complying Innocence;
But knowing where this Ambush lay,
She scap'd the safe, but roughest Way.

lxxxxi
This 'tis to have been from the first
In a Domestick Heaven nurst;
Under the Discipline severe
Of Fairfax, and the starry Vere;
Where not one object can come nigh
But pure, and spotless as the Eye;
And Goodness doth it self intail
On Females, if there want a Male.

lxxxxii

Go now fond Sex that on your Face
Do all your useless Study place,
Nor once at Vice your Brows dare knit
Lest the smooth Forehead wrinkled sit:
Yet your own Face shall at you grin,
Thorough the Black-bag of your Skin;
When knowledge only could have fill'd
And Virtue all of those Furrows till'd.

lxxxxiii

Hence She with Graces more divine
Supplies beyond her Sex the Line;
And, like a sprig of Misleto,
On the Fairfacian Oak does grow;
Whence, for some universal good,
The Priest shall cut the sacred Bud;
While her glad Parents most rejoice,
And make their Destiny their Choice.

lxxxxiv

Mean time ye Fields, Springs, Bushes, Flow'rs,
Where yet She leads her studious Hours,
(Till Fate her worthily translates,
And find a Fairfax for our Thwaites)
Employ the means you have by Her,
And in your kind your selves preferr;
That, as all Virgins She precedes,
So you all Woods, Streams, Gardens, Meads.

lxxxxv

For you Thessalian Tempe's Seat
Shall now be scorn'd as obsolete;
Aranjuez, as less, disdain'd;
The Bel-Retiro as constrain'd;
But name not the Idalian Grove,
For 'twas the seat of wanton Love;

Much less the Deads' Elysian Fields,
Yet nor to them your Beauty yeilds.

lxxxxvi
'Tis not, what once it was, the World;
But a rude heap together hurl'd;
All negligently overthrown,
Gulfes, Deserts, Precipices, Stone.
Your lesser World contains the same.
But in more decent Order tame;
You Heaven's Center, Nature's Lap.
And Paradice's only Map.

lxxxxvii
But now the Salmon-Fishers moist
Their Leathern Boats begin to hoist;
And, like Antipodes in Shoes,
Have shod theyr Heads in their Canoos.
How Tortoise like, but not so slow,
These rational Amphibii go?
Let's in: for the dark Hemisphere
Does now like one of them appear.

The Nymph Complaining for the Death of Her Faun

The wanton Troopers riding by
Have shot my Faun and it will dye.
Ungentle men! They cannot thrive
To kill thee. Thou neer didst alive
Them any harm: alas nor cou'd
Thy death yet do them any good.
I'me sure I never wisht them ill;
Nor do I for all this; nor will:
But, if my simple Pray'rs may yet
Prevail with Heaven to forget
Thy murder, I will Joyn my Tears
Rather than fail. But, O my fears!
It cannot dye so. Heavens King
Keeps register of every thing:
And nothing may we use in vain.
Ev'n Beasts must be with justice slain;
Else Men are made their Deodands.
Though they should wash their guilty hands
In this warm life-blood, which doth part
From thine, and wound me to the Heart,
Yet could they not be clean: their Stain
Is dy'd in such a Purple Grain.
There is not such another in
The World, to offer for their Sin.
    Unconstant Sylvio, when yet
I had not found him counterfeit,
One morning (I remember well)
Ty'd in this silver Chain and Bell,
Gave it to me: nay and I know
What he said then; I'me sure I do.
Said He, look how your Huntsman here
Hath taught a Faun to hunt his Dear.

But Sylvio soon had me beguil'd.
This waxed tame, while he grew wild,
And quite regardless of my Smart,
Left me his Faun, but took his Heart.

Thenceforth I set my self to play
My solitary time away,
With this: and very well content,
Could so mine idle Life have spent.
For it was full of sport; and light
Of foot, and heart; and did invite,
Me to its game: it seem'd to bless
Its self in me. How could I less
Than love it? O I cannot be
Unkind, t' a Beast that loveth me.

Had it liv'd long, I do not know
Whether it too might have done so
As Sylvio did: his Gifts might be
Perhaps as false or more than he.
But I am sure, for ought that I
Could in so short a time espie,
Thy Love was far more better then
The love of false and cruel men.

With sweetest milk, and sugar, first
I it at mine own fingers nurst.
And as it grew, so every day
It wax'd more white and sweet than they.
It had so sweet a Breath! And oft
I blush to see its foot more soft,
And white, (shall I say then my hand?)
NAY any Ladies of the Land.

It is a wond'rous thing, how fleet
'Twas on those little silver feet.
With what a pretty skipping grace,
It oft would challenge me the Race:
And when 't had left me far away,
'Twould stay, and run again, and stay.

For it was nimbler much than Hindes;
And trod, as on the four Winds.

    I have a Garden of my own,
But so with Roses over grown,
And Lillies, that you would it guess
To be a little Wilderness.
And all the Spring time of the year
It onely loved to be there.
Among the beds of Lillyes, I
Have sought it oft, where it should lye;
Yet could not, till it self would rise,
Find it, although before mine Eyes.
For, in the flaxen Lillies shade,
It like a bank of Lillies laid.
Upon the Roses it would feed,
Until its Lips ev'n seem'd to bleed:
And then to me 'twould boldly trip,
And print those Roses on my Lip.
But all its chief delight was still
On Roses thus its self to fill:
And its pure virgin Limbs to fold
In whitest sheets of Lillies cold.
Had it liv'd long, it would have been
Lillies without, Roses within.

    O help! O help! I see it faint:
And dye as calmely as a Saint.
See how it weeps. The Tears do come
Sad, slowly dropping like a Gumme.
So weeps the wounded Balsome: so
The holy Frankincense doth flow.
The brotherless Heliades
Melt in such Amber Tears as these.

    I in a golden Vial will
Keep these two crystal Tears; and fill
It till it do o'reflow with mine;
Then place it in Diana's Shrine.

Now my sweet Faun is vanish'd to
Whither the Swans and Turtles go:
In fair Elizium to endure,
With milk-white Lambs, and Ermins pure.
O do not run too fast: for I
Will but bespeak thy Grave, and dye.

    First my unhappy Statue shall
Be cut in Marble; and withal,
Let it be weeping too: but there
Th' Engraver sure his Art may spare;
For I so truly thee bemoane,
That I shall weep though I be Stone:
Until my Tears, still dropping, wear
My breast, themselves engraving there.
There at my feet shalt thou be laid,
Of purest Alabaster made:
For I would have thine Image be
White as I can, though not as Thee.

An Horatian Ode upon Cromwel's Return
from Ireland

The forward Youth that would appear
Must now forsake his Muses dear,
   Nor in the Shadows sing
   His Numbers languishing.
'Tis time to leave the Books in dust,
And oyl th' unused Armours rust:
   Removing from the Wall
   The Corslet of the Hall.
So restless Cromwel could not cease
In the inglorious Arts of Peace,
   But through adventrous War
   Urged his active Star:
And, like the three-fork'd Lightning, first
Breaking the Clouds where it was nurst,
   Did thorough his own Side
   His fiery way divide.
For 'tis all one to Courage high
The Emulous or Enemy;
   And with such to inclose
   Is more then to oppose.
Then burning through the Air he went,
And Pallaces and Temples rent:
   And Cæsars head at last
   Did through his Laurels blast.
'Tis Madness to resist or blame
The force of angry Heavens flame;
   And, if we would speak true,
   Much to the Man is due:
Who, from his private Gardens, where
He liv'd reserved and austere,
   As if his highest plot
   To plant the Bergamot,

Could by industrious Valour climbe
To ruine the great Work of Time,
    And cast the Kingdoms old
    Into another Mold.
Though Justice against Fate complain,
And plead the antient Rights in vain:
    But those do hold or break
    As Men are strong or weak.
Nature that hateth emptiness,
Allows of penetration less:
    And therefore must make room
    Where greater Spirits come.
What Field of all the Civil Wars
Where his were not the deepest Scars?
    And Hampton shows what part
    He had of wiser Art:
Where, twining subtile fears with hope,
He wove a Net of such a scope,
    That Charles himself might chase
    To Caresbrooks narrow case:
That thence the Royal Actor born
The Tragick Scaffold might adorn,
    While round the armed Bands
    Did clap their bloody hands.
He nothing common did, or mean,
Upon the memorable Scene:
    But with his keener Eye
    The Axes edge did try:
Nor call'd the Gods with vulgar spight
To vindicate his helpless Right,
    But bow'd his comely Head
    Down, as upon a Bed.
This was that memorable Hour
Which first assur'd the forced Pow'r.
    So when they did design
    The Capitols first Line,

A bleeding Head where they begun,
Did fright the Architects to run;
    And yet in that the State
    Foresaw its happy Fate.
And now the Irish are asham'd
To see themselves in one Year tam'd:
    So much one Man can do,
    That does both act and know.
They can affirm his Praises best,
And have, though overcome, confest
    How good he is, how just,
    And fit for highest Trust:
Nor yet grown stiffer with Command,
But still in the Republick's hand:
    How fit he is to sway
    That can so well obey.
He to the Commons Feet presents
A Kingdome, for his first years rents:
    And, what he may, forbears
    His Fame to make it theirs:
And has his Sword and Spoyls ungirt,
To lay them at the Publick's skirt.
    So when the Falcon high
    Falls heavy from the Sky,
She, having kill'd, no more does search,
But on the next green Bow to pearch;
    Where, when he first does lure,
    The Falckner has her sure.
What may not then our Isle presume
While Victory his Crest does plume;
    What may not others fear,
    If thus he crown each Year!
A Cæsar he ere long to Gaul,
To Italy an Hannibal,
    And to all States not free
    Shall Clymacterick be.

The Pict no shelter now shall find
Within his party-colour'd Mind;
    But from this Valour sad
    Shrink underneath the Plad:
Happy if in the tufted brake
The English Hunter him mistake,
    Nor lay his Hounds in near
    The Caledonian Deer.
But thou the Wars and Fortunes Son
March indefatigably on,
    And for the last effect
    Still keep thy Sword erect:
Besides the force it has to fright
The Spirits of the shady Night;
    The same Arts that did gain
    A Pow'r must it maintain.

Tom May's Death

As one put drunk into the Packet-boat,
Tom May was hurry'd hence and did not know't.
But was amaz'd on the Elysian side,
And with an Eye uncertain, gazing wide,
Could not determine in what place he was,
For whence in Stevens ally Trees or Grass.
Nor where the Popes head, nor the Mitre lay,
Signs by which still he found and lost his way.
At last while doubtfully he all compares,
He saw near hand, as he imagin'd Ares.
Such did he seem for corpulence and port,
But 'twas a man much of another sort;
'Twas Ben that in the dusky Laurel shade
Amongst the Chorus of old Poets laid,
Sounding of ancient Heroes, such as were
The Subjects Safety, and the Rebel's Fear,
But how a double headed Vulture Eats
Brutus and Cassius, the Peoples cheats.
But seeing May he varied streight his Song,
Gently to signifie that he was wrong.
Cups more than civil of Emathian wine,
I sing (said he) and the Pharsalian Sign,
Where the Historian of the Common-wealth
In his own Bowels sheath'd the conquering health.
By this May to himself and them was come,
He found he was translated, and by whom.
Yet then with foot as stumbling as his tongue
Prest for his place among the Learned throng.
But Ben, who knew not neither foe nor friend,
Sworn Enemy to all that do pretend,
Rose more than ever he was seen severe,
Shook his gray locks, and his own Bayes did tear
At this intrusion. Then with Laurel wand,

The awful Sign of his supream command,
At whose dread Whisk Virgil himself does quake,
And Horace patiently its stroke does take,
As he crowds in he whipt him ore the pate
Like Pembroke at the Masque, and then did rate:
  'Far from these blessed shades tread back agen
Most servil wit, and Mercenary Pen.
Polydore, Lucan, Allan, Vandale, Goth,
Malignant Poet and Historian both.
Go seek the novice Statesmen, and obtrude
On them some Romane cast similitude,
Tell them of Liberty, the Stories fine,
Until you all grow Consuls in your wine.
Or thou Dictator of the glass bestow
On him the Cato, this the Cicero.
Transferring old Rome hither in your talk,
As Bethlem's House did to Loretto walk.
Foul Architect that hadst not Eye to see
How ill the measures of these States agree.
And who by Romes example England lay,
Those but to Lucan do continue May.
But thee nor Ignorance nor seeming good
Misled, but malice fixt and understood.
Because some one than thee more worthy weares
The sacred Laurel, hence are all these tears?
Must therefore all the World be set on flame,
Because a Gazet writer mist his aim?
And for a Tankard-bearing Muse must we
As for the Basket Guelphs and Gibellines be?
When the Sword glitters ore the Judges head,
And fear has Coward Churchmen silenced,
Then is the Poets time, 'tis then he drawes,
And single fights forsaken Vertues cause.
He, when the wheel of Empire, whirleth back,
And though the World's disjointed Axel crack,
Sings still of ancient Rights and better Times,

Seeks wretched good, arraigns successful Crimes.
But thou base man first prostituted hast
Our spotless knowledge and the studies chaste,
Apostatizing from our Arts and us,
To turn the Chronicler to Spartacus.
Yet wast thou taken hence with equal fate,
Before thou couldst great Charles his death relate.
But what will deeper wound thy little mind,
Hast left surviving Davenant still behind
Who laughs to see in this thy death renew'd,
Right Romane poverty and gratitude.
Poor Poet thou, and grateful Senate they,
Who thy last Reckoning did so largely pay.
And with the publick gravity would come,
When thou hadst drunk thy last to lead thee home.
If that can be thy home where Spencer lyes
And reverend Chaucer, but their dust does rise
Against thee, and expels thee from their side,
As th' Eagles Plumes from other birds divide.
Nor here thy shade must dwell; Return, Return,
Where Sulphrey Phlegeton does ever burn.
Thee Cerberus with all his Jawes shall gnash,
Megæra thee with all her Serpents lash.
Thou rivited unto Ixion's wheel
Shalt break, and the perpetual Vulture feel.
'Tis just what Torments Poets ere did feign,
Thou first Historically shouldst sustain.'
    Thus by irrevocable Sentence cast,
    May only Master of these Revels past.
    And streight he vanisht in a Cloud of pitch,
    Such as unto the Sabboth bears the Witch.

from The Loyal Scot

Prick down the point, whoever has the art,
Where Nature Scotland does from England part.
Anatomists may sooner fix the cells
Where Life resides, or Understanding dwells.
But this we know, though that exceeds our skill,
That whosoever sep'rates them does kill.
    Will you the Tweed that sudden bounder call
Of soyle, of witt, of manners, and of all?
Why draw we not as well the thrifty line
From Thames, Trent, Humber, or at least the Tyne?
So may we the State corpulence redresse,
And little England when we please make lesse.
    What Ethick river is this wondrous Tweed,
Whose one bank virtue, other vice does breed?
Or what new Perpendicular does rise
Up from her stream continu'd to the Skyes,
That between us the common aire should bar
And split the influence of every starre?
But who considers right will find indeed
'Tis Holy-Island parts us, not the Tweed.
Though Kingdomes joyn, yet Church will Kirk oppose:
The Mitre still divides, the Crown does close;
As in Rogation Week, they whip us round
To keep in mind the Scotch and English bound.

The Character of Holland

Holland, that scarce deserves the name of Land,
As but th' Off-scouring of the British Sand;
And so much Earth as was contributed
By English Pilots when they heav'd the Lead;
Or what by th' Oceans slow alluvion fell,
Of shipwrackt Cockle and the Muscle-shell;
This indigested vomit of the Sea
Fell to the Dutch by just Propriety.

Glad then, as Miners that have found the Ore,
They with mad labour fish'd the Land to Shoar;
And div'd as desperately for each piece
Of Earth, as if't had been of Ambergreece;
Collecting anxiously small Loads of Clay,
Less than what building Swallows bear away;
Or than those Pills which sordid Beetles roul,
Transfusing into them their Dunghil Soul.

How did they rivet, with Gigantick Piles,
Thorough the Center their new-catched Miles;
And to the stake a strugling Country bound,
Where barking Waves still bait the forced Ground;
Building their watry Babel far more high
To reach the Sea, than those to scale the Sky?

Yet still his claim the Injur'd Ocean laid,
And oft at Leap-frog ore their Steeples plaid:
As if on purpose it on Land had come
To shew them what's their Mare Liberum.
A daily deluge over them does boyl;
The Earth and Water play at Level-coyl;
The Fish oft-times the Burger dispossest,
And sat not as a Meat but as a Guest;
And oft the Tritons and the Sea-Nymphs saw
Whole sholes of Dutch serv'd up for Cabillau;
Or as they over the new Level rang'd

For pickled Herring, pickled Heeren chang'd.
Nature, it seem'd, asham'd of her mistake,
Would throw their Land away at Duck and Drake.

Therefore Necessity, that first made Kings,
Something like Government among them brings.
For as with Pygmees who best kills the Crane,
Among the hungry he that treasures Grain,
Among the blind the one-ey'd blinkard reigns,
So rules among the drowned he that draines.
Not who first sees the rising Sun commands,
But who could first discern the rising Lands.
Who best could know to pump an Earth so leak
Him they their Lord and Country's Father speak.
To make a Bank was a great Plot of State;
Invent a Shov'l and be a Magistrate.
Hence some small Dyke-grave unperceiv'd invades
The Pow'r, and grows as 'twere a King of Spades.
But for less envy some joynt States endures,
Who look like a Commission of the Sewers.
For these Half-anders, half wet, and half dry,
Nor bear strict service, nor pure Liberty.

'Tis probable Religion after this
Came next in order; which they could not miss.
How could the Dutch but be converted, when
Th' Apostles were so many Fishermen?
Besides the Waters of themselves did rise,
And, as their Land, so them did re-baptize.
Though Herring for their God few voices mist,
And Poor-John to have been th' Evangelist.
Faith, that could never Twins conceive before,
Never so fertile, spawn'd upon this shore:
More pregnant then their Marg'ret, that laid down
For Hans-in-Kelder of a whole Hans-Town.

Sure when Religion did it self imbark,
And from the East would Westward steer its Ark,
It struck, and splitting on this unknown ground,

Each one thence pillag'd the first piece he found:
Hence Amsterdam, Turk-Christian-Pagan-Jew,
Staple of Sects and Mint of Schisme grew;
That Bank of Conscience, where not one so strange
Opinion but finds Credit, and Exchange.
In vain for Catholicks our selves we bear;
The universal Church is onely there.
Nor can Civility there want for Tillage,
Where wisely for their Court they chose a Village.
How fit a Title clothes their Governours,
Themselves the Hogs as all their Subjects Bores!

  Let it suffice to give their Country Fame
That it had one Civilis call'd by Name,
Some Fifteen hundred and more years ago;
But surely never any that was so.

  See but their Mairmaids with their Tails of Fish,
Reeking at Church over the Chafing-Dish.
A vestal Turf enshrin'd in Earthen Ware
Fumes through the loop-holes of a wooden Square.
Each to the Temple with these Altars tend,
But still does place it at her Western End:
While the fat steam of Female Sacrifice
Fills the Priests Nostrils and puts out his Eyes.

  Or what a Spectacle the Skipper gross,
A Water-Hercules Butter-Coloss,
Tunn'd up with all their sev'ral Towns of Beer;
When Stagg'ring upon some Land, Snick and Sneer,
They try, like Statuaries, if they can
Cut out each others Athos to a Man:
And carve in their large Bodies, where they please,
The Armes of the United Provinces.

  But when such Amity at home is show'd;
What then are their confederacies abroad?
Let this one court'sie witness all the rest;
When their whole Navy they together prest,
Not Christian Captives to redeem from Bands:

Or intercept the Western golden Sands:
No, but all ancient Rights and Leagues must vail,
Rather than to the English strike their sail;
To whom their weather beaten Province ows
It self, when as some greater Vessel tows
A Cock-boat tost with the same wind and fate,
We buoy'd so often up their sinking State.

Was this Jus Belli & Pacis; could this be
Cause why their Burgomaster of the Sea
Ram'd with Gun-powder, flaming with Brand wine,
Should raging hold his Linstock to the Mine?
While, with feign'd Treaties, they invade by stealth
Our sore new circumcised Common wealth.

Yet of his vain Attempt no more he sees
Then of Case-Butter shot and Bullet-Cheese.
And the torn Navy stagger'd with him home,
While the Sea laught it self into a foam,
'Tis true since that (as fortune kindly sports,)
A wholesome Danger drove us to our Ports.
While half their banish'd keels the Tempest tost,
Half bound at home in Prison to the frost:
That ours mean time at leizure might careen,
In a calm Winter, under Skies Serene.
As the obsequious Air and Waters rest,
Till the dear Halcyon hatch out all its nest.
The Common wealth doth by its losses grow;
And, like its own Seas, only Ebbs to flow.
Besides that very Agitation laves,
And purges out the corruptible waves.

And now again our armed Bucentore
Doth yearly their Sea-Nuptials restore.
And now the Hydra of seaven Provinces
Is strangled by our Infant Hercules.
Their Tortoise wants its vainly stretched neck;
Their Navy all our Conquest or our Wreck:
Or, what is left, their Carthage overcome

Would render fain unto our better Rome,
Unless our Senate, lest their Youth disuse
The War, (but who would) Peace if begg'd refuse.
    For now of nothing may our State despair,
Darling of Heaven, and of Men the Care;
Provided that they be what they have been,
Watchful abroad, and honest still within.
For while our Neptune doth a Trident shake,
Steel'd with those piercing Heads, Dean, Monk, and Blake,
And while Jove governs in the highest Sphere,
Vainly in Hell let Pluto domineer.

An Epitaph upon Frances Jones

Enough: and leave the rest to Fame.
'Tis to commend her but to name.
Courtship, which living she declin'd,
When dead to offer were unkind.
Where never any could speak ill,
Who would officious Praises spill?
Nor can the truest Wit or Friend,
Without Detracting, her commend.
To say she liv'd a Virgin chaste,
In this Age loose and all unlac't;
Nor was, when Vice is so allow'd,
Of Virtue or asham'd, or proud;
That her Soul was on Heav'en so bent
No Minute but it came and went;
That ready her last Debt to pay
She summ'd her Life up ev'ry day;
Modest as Morn; as Mid-day bright;
Gentle as Ev'ning; cool as Night;
'Tis true: but all so weakly said;
'Twere more Significant, She's Dead.

The Second Chorus from Seneca's Tragedy, *Thyestes*

Stet quicunque volet potens
Aulae culmine lubrico etc.

Climb at Court for me that will
Tottering Favour's slipp'ry hill.
All I seek is to lye still.
Settled in some secret Nest
In calm Leisure let me rest;
And far off the publick Stage
Pass away my silent Age.
Thus when without noise, unknown,
I have liv'd out all my span,
I shall dye, without a groan,
An old honest Country man.
Who expos'd to others Eyes,
Into his own Heart ne'r pry's,
Death to him's a Strange surprise.